CAGE AND AVIARY SERIES

THE
WEST OF ENGLAND FLYING TUMBLER

Other Books Available

Exhibition and Flying Pigeons
Harry G. Wheeler

Pheasants of the World
Dr. Jean Delacour

The Yorkshire Canary
Ernest Howson

Ornamental Waterfowl
Lt. Col. A.A. Johnson and W.H. Payn

Peafowl of the World
Josef Bergmann

The Gloster Fancy Canary
John S. Cross

Poultry Colour Guide
Dr. J. Batty and Charles Francis

Fancy Pigeon Standards
National Pigeon Association

THE

WEST OF ENGLAND

FLYING TUMBLER

By

Jeffrey Oldham

President: **Bristol Tippler and Tumbler Show Society,**
                    Norwich Flying Tippler and Flying Tumbler Society
Vice-President: **West of England Flying Tumbler Society**

Published by

SAIGA PUBLISHING CO. LTD.,
1 Royal Parade, Hindhead, Surrey
GU26 6TD   England.

Typesetting by
Ebony Typesetting, West Tremabe, Nr Liskeard, Cornwall PL14 4LT
Printed and bound by The Pitman Press, Bath

Published by:
SAIGA PUBLISHING CO. LTD.
1 Royal Parade, Hindhead, Surrey, GU26 6TD

ACKNOWLEDGEMENTS

I would like to express my most sincere thanks to the following fanciers, and others, for the loan and gift of photographs and documents and also to Wendy Glynne (Mrs. Ashley Glynne) for assistance with the typing and to John Burn for help with the diagrams. In addition the following have given assistance:

The late Mr. R.S. Ellet, Bristol.
The late Mr. C.A. Hole, Bristol.
Mr. Mel Brooker, Norwich.
Mr. R.E. Connebear, Bideford.
Mr. J.E. Johnson, Scunthorpe.
Mr. M.K. Moore, Norwich.
Mr. J.E. Mullan, Ipswich.
Mr. and Mrs. A. Roscoe, Prescot.
Mr. S.T. Tebbs, Doncaster.

CONTENTS

MONOCHROME ILLUSTRATIONS

The illustrations used in the book show that the breed has changed very little since the early days, although there is now not as much diversity, all modern Wests having the secondary white markings of the Bald Tumbler whatever other marking they may happen to have.

Ludlow, one of whose paintings is reproduced in Figure 1.7, always painted a rather refined bird. The same effect can be produced with the camera, depending on its position in relation to the bird. The only criticism which I have heard of the painting of the Bell Wests is that the beaks are too straight set. A West is slightly downfaced, with the beak pointing somewhat downward towards the ground.

All the modern birds illustrated are Certificate winners and champions and all have won top awards at the Classic shows for the breed.

PREFACE

Of our three native flying breeds, the West of England Flying Tumbler is the only one whose origin, history and development have not been documented. Over the years a number of the older breeders have expressed a wish that I should undertake the task of writing a book on the breed to ensure that what is available in art and the printed word should be preserved.

I have kept and loved the West since I was a boy and youth in the 1930s, so I readily agreed; but although I started to compile these facts and records in 1970, it is only at this much later stage that the project has reached its conclusion.

I am indebted to my many friends and fellow fanciers, some of them now alas passed on, for their opinions and for the gift or loan of articles, paintings and photographs. They are acknowledged in the following pages.

The creative and competitive element which is latent in most people is brought out admirably by a livestock hobby and does as much to enrich our lives as does an interest in music or art or a competitive hobby.

I sincerely hope that my efforts on behalf of our wonderful West of England Flying Tumbler will give you as much pleasure to read as they have given me to compile and write, and that they meet with your approval.

Sychden, N. Wales,   Jeffrey Oldham
February 1980.

Frontispiece **A grouse-legged Blue Bald West of England Flying Tumbler, bred by H. Symonds. From the painting by S. Wiltshire.**
(*Photo:* **C.P.A., Clacton**)

Pair of England Flying Tumbler Blue Print Badges

Bred by H. Symonds

Chapter 1

ORIGIN, HISTORY AND DEVELOPMENT

EARLY DAYS

The **West of England Flying Tumbler*** was developed in Bristol and the West Country in the 1890s and early 1900s. Before this time Flying Tumblers of all types, colours and markings, clean- and grouse-legged as well as grouse- and heavily-muffed birds, had been bred all over the British Isles for at least 200 years: there was a *Standard* for Almond Tumblers as long ago as the early eighteenth century.

The development of the railways and the establishment of agricultural and other shows encouraged the exhibition of **Flying Tumblers**, classified at that time as Long-faced Tumblers to distinguish them from **Almond Tumblers** which were mainly short- or medium-faced birds.

There is documentary evidence that the original British Tumblers were clean-legged and small and that, apart from the Almond, they were found in only the harder colours: **White, Black** and **Blue**. The appearance of muffs and the diversity of size, type and colour found today are due to the infusion of blood from the **Dutch Tumbler**. At this period also, fanciers in

* **Often shortened to "West", a term used later in this book.**

1

Figure 1.1 **Clean-legged Blue West of England Flying Tumbler. Prizewinner in Championship Class at Eastville Fanciers Show, Bristol, 1917. Owner: H. Symonds. From the painting by Andrew Beer.**
(*Photo:* **C.P.A., Clacton**)

3

Birmingham and the Black Country were developing their birds' tumbling and rolling ability and this resulted in today's **Birmingham Roller**.

Avoidance of a Standard

The task of compiling *Standards* began towards the end of the nineteenth century; this led to most Flying Tumblers becoming purely show Tumblers. The Birmingham fanciers, whose birds were usually heavily-muffed, changed these Flying Tumblers over the years into the breed which we know as Muffed Long-faced Tumblers; fanciers elsewhere in the country saw their fliers turn into clean-legged Tumblers with markings designated Bald, Beard, Whiteside and Mottle.

Fortunately, a number of West Country fanciers rejected the idea of breeding their Flying Tumblers to a rigid written *Standard*. They wished to perpetuate their non-standard flying breed in the same way as Racing Homers, Flying Tipplers, Birmingham Rollers and others. They argued that to adopt a *Standard* meant a gradual conversion to a purely exhibition breed, and this view has proved correct with other breeds. We owe the existence of our lovely dual-purpose breed to their wisdom and foresight.

EARLY BREED ORGANISATIONS

The first club to cater for the breed was the City of Bristol **Flying Tumbler Society** which was founded in 1907. Its aims were to preserve the true type of the West and to organise flying competitions and shows. The founder members were Messrs. Ball, Pippen, Millener, Scapens, Harris, Scully, Grant, Notton, James and Balson. The Secretary was Mr. S. Harris and the

Chairman Mr. S. James. Three Old Bird Flies and one Young Bird Fly were held with larger kits than the usual three Tipplers being flown. It would be interesting to speculate whether Tipplers would better the Wests' performance if these larger numbers were to be flown.

If we look at the records over half a century ago we see the following results:

Table of Results					
Event	Result	Owner	No. of birds	Time Hrs.	Mins.
1st Fly	1	Millener	9	10	6
	2	Pippin & Begbie	9	9	40
	3	Harris & Scully	9	9	32
	4	Ball	11	8	28
2nd Fly	1	Harris & Scully	9	8	55
	2	Balson	12	8	25
	3	Boddy	9	9	35
	4	James	13	5	16
3rd Fly	1	Pippin	13	6	40
	2	James	13	6	28
	3	Balson	10	5	28
	4	Ball	11	5	7

There is also a record that a Mr. Vernon flew nine birds for ten hours and nine minutes and eleven birds for nine hours and thirty-two minutes, with other competitors disqualified.

The report of a pre-1949 show quotes the colours and

markings shown as Grizzles, Black, Blue, Mealy, Red, Silver and Chequer Balds, Splashes, Mottles, Spangles, Bell-necks and Saddles, together with Selfs of these colours. The principal winners were Mr. Balson (Grizzle), Mr. Robson (Silver Bald) and Mr. Sillman (Red Spangle).

A grand patron of the breed before World War I was Mr. Bell, a member of a Liverpool family of veterinary chemists. The Bristol agent of the firm was W. Ball who was a prolific writer on the breed and one of Bristol's outstanding breeders.

An example of his writing is reproduced from *The Feathered World Year Book* (1914) and the illustration (Figure 1.2) is from the same source.

> The past year has been a most memorable one in the history of the West fancy, and will undoubtedly stand out prominently in the years to come as an example of what was done in that year to further stimulate interest in these charming high-fliers by that ardent lover of them and great sportsman, Mr. W.H. Bell, whose generosity to the West fancy has been unbounded. His gifts to the City of Bristol Tumbler Flying Society of two ten-guinea Cups — one for old and one for young flying competitions — aroused great interest amongst Bristol fanciers, whilst his further gifts of four two-guinea Cups to an open show promoted by the above Club roused the enthusiasm of all West fanciers, and the finest gathering of these birds was brought together at one show, fanciers sending to compete from such distances as Cornwall and Lancashire, whilst the Welsh fancy was well represented. This revival can be easily understood. My only surprise is that these birds are not taken up far more by fanciers who like real high flying, as undoubtedly they are pre-eminent in that respect, or, to quote our Transatlantic cousins, who say, "As real high-fliers, these Wests are undoubtedly the goods" — a forcible expression to say they are alright.
>
> They require very little training if fed regularly and kept clean, and if flown twice or three times a week, will fly from four to eight hours for the pure love of it without any drilling. I speak as one who has kept a variety over thirty-five years, and may be deemed a crank where Wests are concerned, but my sentiments would be fully endorsed by dozens of West fanciers here in Bristol, the Metropolis of this fancy.

The City of Bristol Tumbler Flying Society held their usual three flies last year, the first being on Whit Monday, when fourteen members competed for Mr. Bell's ten-guinea Cup and Mr. Scapens' Cup. Although the weather was very bad, with heavy rain and wind, yet some good flying was seen. I had the privilege of winning Mr. Bell's Cup for the first time, and Mr. Scapens' for the second time, flying eleven birds 8 hrs. 8 min. In the second old bird fly, for Mr. Edis's Cup, twelve competed, Mr. T. Pippen getting first, flying nine birds 7 hrs. 59 min.; whilst in the young bird fly on August Bank Holiday, for Mr. Bell's ten-guinea Cup and the Club Cup, ten competed, Mr. T. Pippen again got first, flying nine birds 7 hrs. 59 min. This fancier was, unfortunately, disqualified in the first fly through having a bird away at night.

The averages for the three flies are as follows:—

First: Mr. Batson . . . . 7 hrs. 50 min.
Second: Messrs. Harris and Scully . . . . 7 hrs. 5 min.
Third: Mr. S. Bryant . . . . 6 hrs. 49 min.
          Messrs. Boddy and Curtis . . . . 6 hrs. 49 min.

The photo shown is of our Secretary, Mr. G. Harris, and his partner, Mr. Scully, both of whom are very enthusiastic but modest fanciers, whilst our Secretary especially is a good, hard worker for the fancy and most consistent flier. His birds invariably give a good account of themselves, but, as he points out, it is a matter of great difficulty to pick out your best birds for competition, because in his immediate neighbourhood there are so many who fly these birds, and it is no uncommon thing to see a kit of 200 birds flying together. He says, in regard to high and long-time flying, it is the blood that tells. He has a very old race of birds, and has crossed them in very successfully with some of Mr. Batson's strain, which has produced for him more muscular birds. When training for a fly, he separates his birds three weeks before the first competition, and gives the hens which are to be flown a dose of Epsom salts, and for the first week feeds them on barley, flying the birds on alternate days. Second week, a few peas, wheat and tares in the morning, barley at night. The third week, peas, wheat, dari and small maize in the morning, at night barley, wheat and a little canary seed. He gives the birds a drink after each meal, then takes the fountain away; keeps them scrupulously clean, and gives plenty of grit. He says on this treatment he finds the birds fly well.

7

Figure 1.2 **Messrs. Harris and Scully's kit of young birds in 1914. These birds flew for 7 hours and 24 minutes and were second in the August Bank Holiday Match for the Cup at Bristol.**
(*Courtesy: The Feathered World*)

The **West of England Flying Tumbler Society** was formed in the mid-1920s by Mr. W.H. Vodden of Bideford. As he was also the Secretary of the Bideford and Barnstaple Flying Tippler Society there was a very strong link between the two clubs. Both Tippler and West rings were issued, and local societies such as the Eastville (Bristol) Fanciers' Society also issued their own rings. My first pair of Wests consisted of a Black Badge, rung W.E.F.T.S., and a lovely Silver Bald, rung E.F.S. 34-32, which were presented to me by Mr. Vodden. The breed owed its very existence in the period preceding and following World War II to this grand fancier.

In 1949 the Bideford and Barnstaple Flying Tippler Society merged with the Bideford and South West Flying Tippler Society and the W.E.F.T.S. then came under their wing. The Secretary was Mr. Ron Connebear who has done a tremendous job for the breed; Mrs. Connebear exhibits some very nice Wests, especially Creams.

OUTSTANDING FANCIERS AND BREEDERS

In addition to Mr. Vodden, in North Devon Mr. B. Shortbridge, Mr. J. Westacott, Mr. W. Berry, Mr. Stan Lock and others kept the flag flying and their interest is being continued by Mr. Peter Holland and Mr. Ron Tucker.

Among Bristol fanciers, the outstanding breeder between the wars was Mr. W. Jeffries who had a fine stud of Wests which excelled in the air and in the pen. Also notable were Mr. J. Wiltshire and Mr. C. Guest. In the post-war years, Mr. Cliff Hole is probably the outstanding breeder, and Messrs. R.S. Ellett, Colin Monelle and Jim Waters have all made their mark. Mr. J.F. Jones bred exceptionally good Spangles and Badges and these birds are now being bred and exhibited by C. & T.

Hawkins. Another keen devotee of this strain is Alf Williams. Unfortunately, with the death of Stan Savage we have lost one of the most able breeders and judges.

Mr. Logan of London, and later of Parkstone, did much to improve the softer colours and bars. Another enthusiastic supporter on the south coast is Peter Salvage.

Red Spangles have another keen admirer in Mr. Bennett of Reading, while in East Anglia, Melvyn Brooker is a keen supporter of both Red Spangles and Badges. He is now in partnership with Sid Cossey of Norwich, and their team is always to the fore, winning many top honours with the J.F. Jones's strain. In Lincolnshire lives Mr. J.E. Johnson who has probably the largest winning team in the country and who is a wonderful supporter of the breed.

There is a strong contingent of breeders associated with the Suffolk and Essex (Sufex) Columbian Society around the Colchester area. These include Mr. A. Blewitt, Mr. Brian Coulson, Mr. Nelson Sorby and Mr. Gerry Richer. John Burns and Christopher Kiuss are two teenagers who work very hard for the Society. Mr. R.C. Hall, the prominent breeder of Holle Croppers and Secretary of the Breed Club has recently acquired some good Black Bald Wests.

In Worcester, Mr. Vic Zalnicke breeds some very fine Black and Red Bald Wests, and Lancashire is fortunate to have Alan and Mary Roscoe as leading exhibitors, while Ted Evans also pens some very fine Wests. In Yorkshire, we have Mr. S.T. Tebbs of Doncaster, a very successful breeder and exhibitor, who now writes alternate West notes in *Pigeons and Pigeon World*, and Mr. H. Clayton of Bradford.

EARLY DESCRIPTIONS OF TUMBLERS

Before proceeding further, it is useful to examine the early descriptions of the older types of Tumbler which existed when the West of England was being developed. James C. Lyell, in *Pigeon-Keeping for Amateurs* (1892), describes Tumblers and the methods of management as shown below:

> The Tumbler pigeon exists in great variety throughout the world, and is everywhere a favourite. It derives its name from an inherited capability of turning somersaults in the air. Willoughby, the English ornithologist, writing more than two hundred years ago, describes the Tumbler as "small and of divers colours. They have strange motions, turning themselves backwards over their heads, and show like footballs in the air."
>
> The general appearance of the everywhere well-known and common flying and performing Tumbler is that of a full-breasted, short-legged pigeon weighing from 10 ounces to 12 ounces. The head is rounded rather than angular; the beak is short compared with that of the common blue or chequered dove-cote pigeon; the iris of the eye ought to be of a pearl white, though generally more or less reddish round the outer circumference, while many good performing birds have yellow or gravel eyes, and others hazel, or, in fanciers' language, "bull" eyes. The flight and tail feathers are of medium length, and the legs and feet unfeathered. This type of pigeon is found in infinite variety of colouring, such as all blue, silver, black, dun, red, yellow, and white, also marked in some way or other with white, such as white-flighted or white-tailed, or mottled over the body more or less with white. There are also chequers of various colours, as well as grizzles, the latter having the fibres of the webs of the feathers a mixture of white and colour, such as blue-grizzle and red-grizzle. In short, the variation in colour and marking of a the common Tumbler is so extensive that it would not be difficult to select, out of a dealer's stock, in the course of a year, a hundred birds no two of which would be alike. This arises from breeding the best flying and performing birds together regardless of colour. At the same time there were, not long ago, various breeds of Tumblers that could perform well in the air, which have been long bred for colour and marking, such as the Macclesfield Tippler, black, blue, and silver Beards, and Baldpates of various colours. These were good tumbling birds in former days, but I fear that the well-marked Beards, Balds, and

12

Mottles so extensively bred nowadays for the show-pen are not, in many cases at least, Tumblers in anything but name. In fact, the majority of them, including the rich-coloured black, red, and yellow self-coloured birds one sees at every pigeon show, are merely "toy" pigeons, some of which have been crossed with non-tumbling breeds to produce good colour.

The tumbling propensity of the Tumbler is inherited, and what causes it to turn over in its flight is not known. Some pure-bred ones never attain to it, and others may be seen trying to turn over, but only getting half way. While young, and before they get proficient, they make many such attempts to turn a complete somersault. One style of tumbling is to give one turn at a time, and that so quickly that the bird does not lose way in its flight. Others come to a stop in their flight, clap their wings, and then make a single, double, or treble somersault. The Roller, again, will come down twenty or thirty feet through the air, rise again, and execute a succession of such performances, when he is entitled to be called a "long" Roller. Many good birds have been killed through their inability to stop tumbling till they reached the ground. Now and then a bird is produced from a good stock of Tumblers that is unable to rise a yard from the ground without tumbling. From such birds a breed has been produced called "house," "parlour", or "ground" Tumblers, which tumble when flying about in a small aviary, or which, in some cases, are unable to leave the floor of their loft without tumbling back on the ground.

The Tumbler fancier who is attached to his birds must devote much time and attention to them, as they require special care and training, without which they deteriorate in regard to flying. They must not be allowed unlimited freedom, or they will get into a habit of sitting about chimney-tops and roofs, instead of mounting into the clouds. Those also that leave the flight and cause the others to descend must be weeded out. They are generally flown in the morning and then confined for the rest of the day. Those that fly very high, and for some hours at a time, generally tumble only when rising and descending. Of late years the records of some extraordinary Tumbler-flying have been published. At the Nottingham and Leicester summer matches, the winning flights have been on the wing for as long as thirteen hours. The birds that do this, however, are not always pure Tumblers, but Cumulet-bred pigeons.

The **Cumulet**, or **Volant**, a bird of extraordinary power of

13

flight, is of French or Flemish origin. It is much the same size as a Tumbler, generally white, or white with red ticked neck, and with a pure white iris, or "fish eye" as it is called.

A variety of Tumbler, not so generally kept as the clean-legged kind just described, is the feather-legged or "muffed" breed, much fancied about Birmingham and the Midlands. These birds are generally longer-beaked and rather larger than the others and with feathered legs and feet varying from grouse-legged to long-muffed, some of them having foot-feathering 4in. in length. Such as are bred for the show-pen will be described further on. Many of these muffed Tumblers, when bred for flying and tumbling regardless of feather, are described as good performers, affording great enjoyment to the numerous fanciers who keep them.

The **Macclesfield Tippler** is an old breed of clean-legged Tumbler, and was formerly noted for its rapid tumbling and high flying, generally making single turns in its flight. The colour known as "printed" in this breed is white with dark points, the head, flight, and tail being brownish-black with more or less mottling over the neck and body.

Long-faced Tumblers for the show-pen are now very extensively bred, and though not long-faced in comparison with some pigeons are so called to distinguish them from the real short-faced, such as the Almond. The Long-faced Tumbler for the show-pen should have all the shape and make of the best type of flying bird, be pearl-eyed, have very little beak and eye-wattle, and not so short a beak as to appear to have any cross of the real Short-faced, or it becomes what is called "pleasant" faced. In whole or self colour it is shown black, red, yellow, and white, and occasionally blue and silver. Depth of colour, accompanied with metallic lustre on the feather, is the desideratum, after correct type, in these birds. The rarest to see good is the red, which seldom carries its colour to the end of the tail.

Mottles and **Rosewings** are identical with the foregoing except in marking. The Rosewing should have a rose pinion of single white feathers, well separated from each other, on the shoulders of each wing, lying in a round form, or within the compass of a circle the size of a crown-piece. The Mottle, in addition to such a rose pinion, should have a V shaped mottling of single, well-separated, white feathers on the back: this is known as a "handkerchief" back, and is rarely seen good. Both these varieties are extremely difficult to breed anything like perfect. In

14

breeding them — and they exist in black, red, and yellow — birds are produced with too much or with no marking. Self colours, mottle-bred, are, however, useful to breed from. It is evident that the standard of perfection in Mottles and Rose-wings is one peculiarly open to fraudulent practices in the way of clipping out foul feathers. Whole-coloured birds have won prizes as Rose-wings, the mottling having been added by cutting off some feathers near the skin and inserting white feathers into their shafts. A few white Rosewings have been lately produced; these are white with a rose pinion of black feathers.

Figure 1.3 **Mottle Tumbler**

The **Whiteside Tumbler** exists in red and yellow, and ought to be all coloured except on the shoulders, being in marking the reverse of the Turbit pigeon. These birds do not come out of the nest so marked, but assume the white shoulders during their first moult. They are apt to fail in strength of colour in flights, tail, and on the lower parts of the body.

The **Almond Tumbler** (Long-faced) is sometimes found very good in colour with the rich yellow ground so desirable in the Short-faced Almond. Good flying and tumbling Almonds formerly existed.

The **Baldhead** or **Baldpate Tumbler** exists in black, blue, silver, red and yellow. The marking that looks best is when the white runs in a straight line about $\frac{1}{8}$ in. below the eye. The flights ought to be white to the turn, or "ten and ten a side" as it is called: the rump and tail with its coverts should be white and the whole of the underbody the same. The line of demarcation below the breast is called the "belt", and ought to be in a straight line. Pearl eyes are requisite in Baldheads for exhibition; but in breeding them odd-eyed and bull-eyed birds are often produced. The best birds are blues and blacks, very few really good coloured reds and

15

yellows being in existence. Good tumbling and high-flying Baldheads once existed, and beautiful they looked on the wing, their white points telling well as they wheeled in their flight. They are serviceable feeders for Short-faced Tumblers.

Beard Tumblers are also found in all the chief colours, and pretty birds they are when well marked. They derive their name

Figure 1.4 **Baldhead Tumbler**

from a dash of white under the beak extending from eye to eye as shown in Fig. 1.5. The upper mandible should be coloured and the lower one white; the eyes should be pearl-white and not dull or dusky; the tail, with its coverts, and the ten primary flights of each wing should be white and the rest of the plumage coloured; but the feathers on the lower part of the thighs adjoining the hocks are generally more or less white. The black, blue, and Silver Beards of thirty years ago could fly and tumble well, but most of those exhibited now are mere toys bred for the show-pen.

Figure 1.5 **Beard Tumbler**

Muffed Tumblers exist in whole-feathered black, white, red, yellow, blue, silver, and chequered; and also in Mottles and Rosewings. The feathers on their legs and feet should be as long as

16

possible, and appear like small wings. What are called **Saddles** and **Badges** have probably the same origin, but the marking differs. The Saddle, found mostly in blue and black, was said formerly to be a muff-legged Tumbler marked exactly the same as a Magpie Pigeon, but the present standard is that of the Magpie with some white marking about the head as follows: a white snip or narrow line from the beak-wattle to the forehead about $\frac{1}{2}$in. long, a white spot or narrow line about $\frac{1}{4}$in. long over each eye, and an extensive white beard under the beak from eye to eye on which two coloured spots, called "Whiskers", extend from the wicks of the mouth downwards and backwards. Badges also have these head-markings, but with the exception of white primary flights and white leg and foot feathering, from the hocks downward, are all coloured. Saddles and Badges are rarely seen well marked, and are not much fancied outside of the Midlands. Their breeders are not yet unanimous as to what constitutes correct head-markings.

DEVELOPMENT OF THE WEST

The evolution of the **West** from the end of the last century to the present day has been gradual. The **Flying Tippler** evolved from the original Flying Tumblers, although other breeds such as the **Cumulet** have been used. Even today there are strains which can fly as long as nineteen hours; these are referred to as **Tumbler-type Tipplers** and are often Bald-marked with white flights and tails. The ideal Tippler was always considered to be the **Macclesfield** which had the Light Print or Mottle marking in either Black on White or Dun on White. These birds no doubt had Cumulet or Tumbler ancestry.

The **Manchester Tippler**, on the other hand, was believed to have a lot of the old **Short-faced Tumbler** in its makeup, from which it inherited its mottled, greasy, Almond-like colouring and its tendency to dropped flights.

Figure 1.6 **A champion Light Print Tippler hen. Bred and exhibited by Harold Williamson of Hamsterley, Co. Durham.**
The Tippler is a small to medium sized bird, head fairly round, with shortish, dark beak and dark flights and tail. It is quite distinct now from the oval-headed, long-beaked West with its white flights and tail.

18

Up to World War II the Tippler was regarded as a dual-purpose bird, with **Macclesfield Prints** and **Mottles** winning competitions with times of seventeen to eighteen hours and also winning in the show pen, but as flying times increased to nineteen to twenty hours, special strains of competition Tippler were produced, so that the dual-purpose bird vanished from the scene. In the same way Tipplers bred for the show pen improved, ousting the competition Tipplers, so that we now have two strains of Tippler, one for flying and one for the show-pen.

Immediately before and after World War I, the various agricultural shows began to include in their pigeon schedules classes for Flying Tumblers. At this period, Wests were clean-legged, grouse-legged or grouse-muffed. Markings other than Bald, such as Spangles, Red-necked, Bell-necked, etc, were almost entirely of the clean-legged or grouse-legged variety, and there were Selfs in various colours with dark tails and flights. Most of the darker colours had coloured flights and tails, and dark beaks as well in many instances. These continued to be exhibited until World War II.

Not only was there great variety in the **Wests**, but in the Flying Tumbler classes were also to be found Birmingham Rollers and ordinary clean-legged Flying Tumblers. The latter must not be confused with **Wests**, and although they are quite good Tumblers in the air, they are quite distinct also from Birmingham Rollers, being much larger, and very robust, compact and strong in appearance, like a big strong Tippler with the same round head and a shortish, strong beak of a horn or dark colour.

After World War I, the Self Wests disappeared and the Bristol Flying Tumbler Society ceased to function; but still Rollers, Wests and Flying Tumblers continued to compete against each other in Flying Tumbler classes. Very soon, in the early 1920s, the Roller fanciers began to get themselves organised and ceased to compete in these classes, but one or two common clean-legged Flying Tumblers continued to be exhibited until the late 1920s or early '30s, by which time the Wests, with their good type, superb bodies and silky feathers, won the day so that they alone competed in the Flying Tumbler classes. In the last decade the classes have been designated for West of England Flying Tumblers.

In the early 1920s, the **West of England Flying Tumbler Society** assumed the functions of the defunct Bristol Flying Tumbler Society and began the task of agreeing a fixed type for their birds, so securing the future for a non-standard *West of England High and Long-Flying Tumbler*, as it was called at first. As it has only been recently that the breed has received its correct title, even younger fanciers with only ten or twelve years' experience have seen part of the evolution process.

While corn was rationed during and after World War II, West studs became very depleted, in common with other breeds, and the dark-tailed, dark-beaked birds disappeared. Later in the 1950s, the clean- and grouse-legged birds also disappeared, **so that we now have only grouse-muffed birds competing in West classes.**

Position in U.S.A.

As far as I know, America is the only country which has imported Wests, many good birds having been sent there in the 1930s. Unfortunately, American fanciers have decided to have two types and have adopted two *Standards*: one for the West of England Flying Tumbler and one for what they call a West of England Show Tumbler. This resembles more closely a Muffed Tumbler than a West, and the older West fanciers were quite indignant about this, considering that this bird should be called by any name rather than West of England Tumbler — I believe

Figure 1.7 **A pair of Black Bald High and Long-flying West of England Tumblers belonging to Mr. W.H. Bell. From the painting by Ludlow, 1909.**

(*Photo:* **C.P.A., Clacton**)

23

Figure 1.8 **A pair of Blue Chequer Bald West of England Flying Tumblers. Owned by the author. From the painting by W.F. Cooke, 1977.**

(*Photo:* **C.P.A., Clacton**)

that 'American Show Tumbler' has been suggested. However, the West of England Flying Tumbler seems to be a very popular breed in the States, with a strong club and large entries at shows. It remains to be seen whether in time it will change to a purely fancy breed as has always happened in this country when a *Standard* has been adopted for a flying breed.

Only one type in U.K.

Since some less experienced fanciers, writers and observers seem to be under the impression that there are two types in this country — one for flying and one for the show-pen — it must be said now that this is entirely wrong. It is true that a fancier may get rid of stock which he does not consider to be up to show pen standard to other fanciers or to beginners for flying; others, who may or may not fly their stock, may describe Wests which they have for sale as "show quality Wests" or just "show Wests", but none of this must be taken to imply that there are two types.

In this country there is only one type of West of England Flying Tumbler, and the same bird can be a good high flier *and* win in the show-pen even in the classic shows for the breed. To say that it cannot be done is just nonsense.

SUMMARY

The modern West of England Tumbler has taken more than eighty years to develop into its present form. Its main characteristics or features are as follows:

1. A dual purpose breed suitable for flying or exhibition.
2. The breed is now "grouse-muffed", which means the legs are feathered to a moderate degree.

3. Wests fly very high and for long periods so they become specks in the sky. They turn or tumble occasionally and then rejoin the group (the "kit").
4. They combine excellent flying abilities with splendid feathering and condition.

Wests are fascinating birds; they provide competition, interest in the many colours available, and a challenge to produce good performers as well as show birds.

Chapter 2

TYPE, MARKINGS AND COLOURS

DESCRIPTION

The early fanciers in Bristol rejected the idea of a *Standard* when they formed their club in the early 1900s, but the West should comprise all the correct Tumbler and Flying characteristics. The following description embodies my own views on type, but at the end of this chapter I have included the opinions of other people so that the reader may make his own objective appraisal.

Size	Medium and nicely balanced; not too high or low on the leg.
Carriage	Alert and erect, with the head vertically above the feet.
Head	"Pleasant-faced", i.e. rising gradually from wattle to a nice curve over the eye, with no suggestion of full cheeks, blending into the neck; wedge-shaped when viewed from the front.
Beak	Spindle-shaped; light or flesh colour.
Wattle	Light or flesh colour.

Eyes   Pearl or white (i.e. small black pupil with broad, light coloured iris). Position to be as central in the head as possible, when viewed from the side.

Cere   Light or flesh coloured.

Neck   Of medium length.

Chest   Full and symmetrical.

Legs   Grouse-muffed, footings ideally 1-1½ inches. Excessive muffs as in Muffed Tumblers are absolutely wrong.

Wings   Of good length, opening out into a perfect curve with no stepping at the extremities of the flights. The wing coverts and pinion feathers should be even in formation, and the under-furnishings full, complete and even, not ragged in formation.

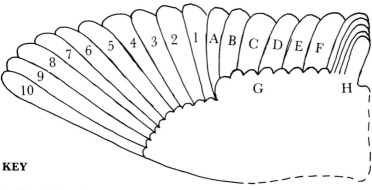

KEY

1—10   Main primary flight feathers. These should be fairly broad with good quality webbing and strong flexible quills.

A—F   Secondaries. These again should be broad, of good silky texture, well overlapping and covering the back.

G   Wing Coverts   H   Pinion Feathers

Figure 2.1   **Diagram of typical wing.**

29

Figure 2.2 **Wing structure. Diagram of a Cream Bald with details of wing structure.**

There are three muscles which control the movement of the wing. The first of these is the **great pectoral** or breast muscle which is used to depress the wing. This is triangular in shape and is attached to the keel and the side of the breast bone; its fibres forming a wide, flat tendon which is attached to the humerus. The second pectoral muscle, which is the elevator of the wing, is placed deep in the flesh and is covered by the great pectoral. This muscle is attached to the keel and passes to the back of the shoulder joint where it is also attached to the humerus.

The third pectoral muscle, which also assists in depressing the wing, connects the breast bone to the humerus and is of similar shape to the great pectoral. From this is can be readily understood that a flying pigeon must always have an abundance of firm flesh and muscle and why, even in the show pen, a good judge wants to feel a West that handles like a new tennis ball rather than a soft orange.

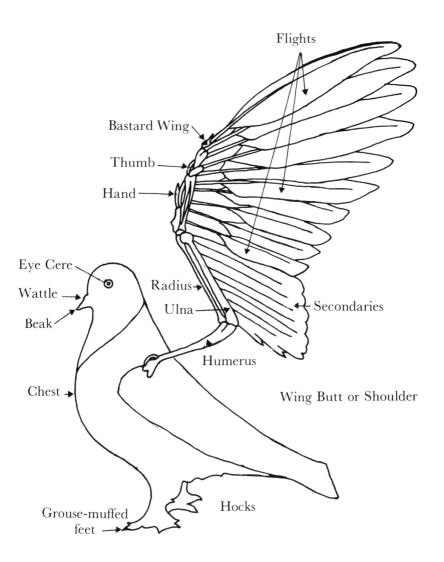

Flights

Bastard Wing

Thumb

Hand

Eye Cere

Wattle

Beak

Radius

Ulna

Secondaries

Chest

Humerus

Wing Butt or Shoulder

Grouse-muffed
feet

Hocks

Tail Straight and of good length with twelve tightly folded feathers. It should fan out into an even curve and be fully covered with furnishings under as well as over, the tail coverts being complete and even. The retrices should be fairly broad and fold to a width of one or two feathers, extending about $\frac{1}{2}$ - $\frac{3}{4}$ inch beyond the extremity of the flights.

Plumage A wealth of silky feathers with strong, broad flights should cover the back, both when the wing is closed and when it is extended in the hand.

Colours and Markings

Wests can be of any colour or marking. In the early days of the breed they were to be found as Self colours with coloured flights and tails, or as Badges with coloured tails, but today all Wests have the secondary white markings of the Bald Long-faced Tumbler on the flights and tail, with a white rump, under-belly, stockings and muffs.

The most popular marking is the Bald, which in the West is typically a long, sloping 'V', rather than the high cut 'V' of the Bald Long-faced Tumbler. It may be either chequered or whole coloured and is found in Red, Yellow, Black, Dun, Blue, Silver, Cream, Mealy, Lavender, Bronze and Strawberry. My own favourite is the Blue Chequered Bald.

Spangles and Splashes may have the V-nicked Bald marking or the Badge marking on the head, and there are also a few Saddles and Bell-necks around, but nowadays these markings are usually only seen on Red-coloured birds. Birds with coloured markings on the head whose body colour is too solid for Spangles are classed as Badges.

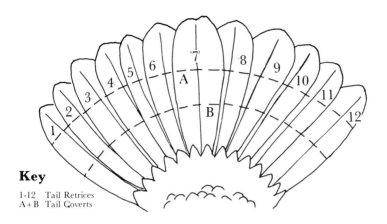

Key

1-12   Tail Retrices
A + B   Tail Coverts

Figure 2.3   **Diagram of spread tail.**
Although some flying pigeons have more than twelve main tail feathers or retrices, the native flying breeds should possess no more than this number and most judges would penalise a bird with more than the usual number.

Colour Description

Red	Blood red
Yellow	The dilute of Red. Should be a rich golden colour.
Mealy	Varies from a pale colour to Strawberry, always with red or reddish bars. The lighter mealy or creamy white shade is preferable, the red bars then looking very attractive; particularly when the bird's appearance is further enhanced by a frosty, sparkling hackle.
Cream	The dilute of Mealy; a creamy biscuit colour, always with a darker or a yellow bar.
Blue	A clear blue, with black bars, free from any slatey shade.

33

Figure 2.4 **Blue Chequer Bald hen, a noted winner including Best in Show All Breeds. Owned by the author.**

(*Photo:* **A.J. Marston, London**)

Silver	The dilute of Blue; a very pale, silvery grey with black bars. (These are, in fact, a very dark brown, bordering on black.) A bird with brown or dun bars is classed as a Silver Dun, which in some breeds is the term used to describe a dunnish body with darker dun or brown bars.
Black	A good jet black with a beetle-like sheen on the hackles, particularly in the cock.
Dun	The dilute of Black; a tan colour which can vary from a light shade almost to bronze.

Off Colours

Strawberry	Generally a faded Red.
Bronze	May be the result of a cross between a Red and a Black.
Lavender	Usually a pale Strawberry or may be genetically a barless Silver.

Many of the off colours seem to fail in the eye, particularly the Strawberries.

Loss of Colour

Mating together for several generations the softer colours such as Yellow and Cream results in faded colours such as washy, pale Yellows and near-white Creams. Most important of all, the bars fade into near-extinction. The remedy for this situation is to mate a Red cock to a Yellow hen, and either a Mealy or Blue cock to a Cream hen, which will rapidly produce again the rich golden Yellows and good coloured Creams with distinct yellow bars.

Grizzles

It is not really correct to call Grizzle a colour, although many pigeon schedules do so. The birds have a "pepper and salt" appearance but, being genetically Blue showing a dark bar, it is more accurate to call it a colour pattern. An anology from another breed is that some Frill-backs are Red Grizzles.

Genetically, the pattern is caused by a dominant factor, and in most breeds of pigeon is produced by a Grizzle x Blue mating when all the progeny will be Grizzles. If they are continually mated together then, like the Creams and Yellows, they will tend to fade.

Technically, a Grizzle is a bird that has two colours, generally blue and white or red and white, appearing on the same feather. A bird would be described as a **Light** or **Dark Grizzle** according to the proportion of white to the darker colour. Some years ago this colour was frequently seen, but today it is very rare, although one breeder is now trying to revive it.

Tortoiseshell and **Almond** varieties are, sadly, no longer seen in the West. Both the latter had three colours appearing on each feather of the bird. In the case of the Tortoiseshell, the colours were red, blue and white and for the Almond, almond, black and white.

Many fanciers, particularly those with Racing Homers, call any faded colour a Grizzle. They are usually referring to all-white or near-white birds with the Print marking on the head and neck. In both pigeons and poultry this is quite a common marking, with white bodies and black hackles, flights and tail. Tipplers marked in this manner are known as Light or Dun Prints; Sussex poultry are called Light Sussex. They are, however, the heaviest birds used to produce egg-laying hybrids, so this is probably an abbreviation for Light Print Sussex, although the equivalent Wyandotte is called a Columbian Wyandotte.

Figure 2.5 **Champion Red Spangled cock, the winner of many prizes and N.P.A. Certificates. Bred and exhibited by Cossey & Brooker (Norwich).**

(*Photo:* **J.E. Mullan, Ipswich**)

OTHER DESCRIPTIONS OF TYPE

City of Bristol Flying Tumbler Society

Although the members rejected the idea of a *Standard* they circulated the following description of the breed:

> The West should be medium in size, weight around 12oz. The body should be round, slightly long cast in wings and tail, but with a round broad chest tapering away like a wedge. Legs of medium length; clean-legged, slightly lower on leg than muffed legged to retain balanced appearance. Shoulders not prominent, but not tucked in with a humped back appearance. Shoulders with a slight rise to give a slightly hollow-backed appearance. Neck of medium length but broad at base blending well into the body. Head fairly long and oval with the highest point over the eye which should be clear pearl with a small black pupil and broad white iris. The eye to be placed as near central of the head as possible, cheeks flat, long spindle beak. The West should carry a wealth of feather of a soft silky nature; flights long and broad with strong quills, well lapping web and carried on tail. Tail feathers broad and strong, well carried slightly beyond flights. The West should handle firm in body with a long keel that is not too deep. Any colour or marking is permissible.

W.H. Vodden (1948)

> The correct type is broad at the shoulders, bold square front going away like a wedge and pearl eyed. Colour is a secondary matter. One should first of all look for the type, hardness of the body and silky feather. Let us retain the West type and feel the handling as one would have in a Flying Tippler.

C.A. Hole (1948)

This description was written shortly after a visit to the 1947 Bideford Show when the fortunes of the breed were at a low ebb and it was struggling for its existence during the corn rationing which followed World War II:

> To see a kit of Wests high up in the sky rocking back and forth with occasional routing and tumbling is indeed a pretty sight and one I am afraid very rare. Unfortunately, they receive little attention these days.

Wests have white flights and tail, the head is usually white with the white coming to a V down the throat. Body colours are many; blue, black, silver, yellow, cream, strawberry, dun, mealy, red, spangle and chequer.

The head is of medium size and the curve of the skull is oval with a high broad forehead showing no marked flatness, acute angles or indentations. The eye is pearl with white iris and black pupil. The cere is small and fine in texture and it is flesh coloured in all varieties.

Wing bars should be distinct, the flights should be carried over and reaching almost to the end of the tail. The body is medium sized, wedge shaped, with broad shoulders and cobby about the chest; the whole being supported by legs well set and of medium length. The feet are small, moderately muffed and the carriage is sprightly, upright and jaunty. This adds to their alertness, vigour and beauty.

Mel Brooker (1979)

This recent description is written by a breeder who, in partnership with Sid Cossey, has won many top awards at leading shows for the breed:

Let us first look at the overall balance and the handling of the West. As with any flying breed, they must come to the hand and be properly balanced. First we must have a good length of keel running the full length of the body and not suddenly stopping off two-thirds the length but tapering to the vent. Short keeled birds are bad handling birds, and most will drop their tails and be unbalanced in the hand, also birds that are either too deep or too shallow in the keel will be uncomfortable in the hand and will usually drop their wings to try and balance themselves. So the first thing we must look for is a good handling and well balanced bird in the hand, wide at the front, tapering off nicely to the tail, keeping its tail together and straight as if one feather. Don't worry too much about the overall length of the bird as I've seen top class birds which are both long casted and short casted, but bear in mind when pairing such birds as it's much better to have the happy medium.

Next let's take a look at the real quality of feather, as no flying breed is worth its salt without feather. The primary wing flights should be of good width and strength, with the strong quill to carry such a feather. Many birds are lacking in this respect, but it can be the difference between a winner and an also-ran in top condition. The secondary flights should also be of the same quality. The secondary covert feathers should also as implied cover the rump of the bird so as not to see the bird's back. This is one of the real finer points and perhaps ignored by many fanciers because it is hard to get. This will give the bird a much better overall effect when viewed through the pens. Thus the reason that birds with good covering will take top honours over birds which lack it, after taking all other finer points into account.

I should think that one of the most striking things about the West Tumbler is the head and eye. The head when viewed from the side should be more oval in shape than round, with a nice rise from the wattle sweeping back over the head with no flat appearance. The wattle should be fine and not too large or coarse. The beak should be long but no spindle or too short, but giving a pleasant look; bold expression in cocks and sweet look in hens is what I always look for. I must admit I don't mind cocky looking hens, but I frown on henny looking cocks, which goes for many breeds. The eye in most colours leaves little to desire these days although we still see some birds a little better than others, particularly in certain colours. The real pearl eye is still hard to get on some of the red and ash reds such as strawberry and mealy balds. Also in these particular colours the eye usually takes longer to develop and I would advise to run the birds on for over a year to see the full effect of colour change in the eye, this can apply to some other colours also. What often appears as a bad eyed youngster can and will make a good eyed adult.

Now for the legs, I like to see a low leg placement with good footings. I speak for most fanciers when I say that most of us don't like to see long legged Wests. Many birds adopt a crouching position in the pen, this makes it harder to see if they are in fact leggy birds. The footings should be of medium length and right down to the toes, covering these.

Now for the markings. Many newcomers seem to have it in their minds that a West should be bald marked with 10 x 10 white flights and nothing else*. The fact is the West comes in many markings such as badges, and I don't mean mismarked balds, bell-necks, saddle-backs, oddsides, and of course the spangle which are splashed all over. These are all accepted in the show

* **Editorial note: This comment is interesting because even some judges look for this feature.**

pen and many of these other marked birds have won *Best in Show* awards at the classic shows. I advise, therefore, not to worry too much regarding the markings, but breed for type and quality. One can still keep the bird to which you are attracted whether it be the bald or othermarked, but please don't be afraid to show the othermarked birds as they do win.

Fulton's Book of Pigeons

This book was published about a century ago, before the advent of the Long-faced Tumbler. At that time reference was made chiefly to common and Flying Tumblers, with some mention being made of the Short-faced Tumbler. Of interest is this description of the Flying Tumbler:

> There are certain peculiarities which enable a good judge to arrive at a pretty accurate assumption, and upon handling a bird it is not an uncommon thing to hear it said "Ah, here is a good one." This remark applies in great measure to the narrow span around the stern of the bird, and the fullness and extra weight at the front, where the chief motive power is wanted. The principal points are width of shoulder, shortness of back and narrowness of rump. The size of the bird is say medium, for there is always a danger in either extreme. The body, round and plump, and the actual outline when bereft of feathers presents nearly a triangular form. The head is high in front, the beak of spindle character, thin and dove shaped though not long, but pleasant faced as they are called. The eye prominent and of a pearly white colour; neck short and of a sudden taper; breast full and prominent; back short; legs of moderate length (in muffed leg they are longer but appear about the same); feet rather small. The temperament of these birds is quiet and contented.

Chapter 3

BREEDING

One of the differences between the breeders of Wests and those of other fancy varieties like the Long-faced Tumblers is that the latter tend to specialise in one colour and marking while the former keep a variety and, therefore, have only one or two pairs of any particular colour to mate.

CUSTOMARY MATINGS

Spangles and **Badges** are usually mated together. The **Bald** marked birds are normally kept in a separate stud with just an occasional mating with the other markings.

Of the Balds, **Blacks** are often mated together; if another colour is introduced it is usually a Black-bred Strawberry or Bronze. **Reds** are also mated together, or a Red mated to a Yellow to improve the colour of the Yellow progeny.

It is advisable to mate **Bars** together. **Blues** can be mated with their own colour or with any other Bar. Recessive colours such as **Silver** should be mated together or a Silver cock mated to a hen of a dominant Bar colour, such as a Blue. Some breeders cross **Yellows** with soft Bars, such as Creams, but I prefer to cross them with Reds and then mate the Bars together.

Chequers, which are usually Reds, Blues, Silvers or Duns, can be mated together or with Reds or Bars, preferably birds which are not too dark a colour.

It is better to mate **Spangles** or **Red Splashes** together or with Badges or Saddles, with just an occasional cross with Balds to give hybrid vigour and colour. The older breeders always crossed a Black, perhaps a Badge or a mismarked Bald, into their Red Spangles or Splashes.

BREEDING FOR QUALITY

Try to mate best with best and avoid if at all possible mating together birds with the same fault. If a certain point is lacking in a stud it is usually advisable to use a bird which excells in that particular quality even if it is lacking in other directions.

For example, a bird may be too much on the leg or too large, but it may have the wealth of feather or the head and eye which you require, so you should use it for these qualities rather than discard it for its faults.

A fancier who flies his Wests will put more emphasis on flying ability and common sense than the fancier whose birds are bred mainly for the show pen, and he would tend to discard those which are larger than average as they are usually the first to drop.

THE BREEDING SEASON

When the show season has finished, then the breeding season commences; fanciers usually mate their birds between January and March. I always show my birds towards the end of the show season in late January and early February, and then mate my birds in mid-February.

Figure 3.1   **The author's champion Silver Bald Hen. Best in Show, 1st and N.P.A. Certificate, Ellet and Logan Trophies: West of England Flying Tumbler Society CH Show, Bideford; 1st N.P.A. Certificate, Best West: National Tippler Union CH Show, Worcester; 1st N.P.A. Certificate, Bath West: Edinburgh International CH Show.**

(*Photo:* **A.J. Marston, London**)

Ringing

All young birds should be rung when they are about eight days old. Care must be taken that the ring cannot slip off and get lost in the nest litter; in some cases it may be better to delay ringing for another day or so.

BREEDING PRINCIPLES

The questions of colour breeding and sex-linkage are often misunderstood by pigeon fanciers so at this point it may be useful to explain the principles fully but simply.

My experience of breeding sex-linked poultry crosses and hybrids and of sexing day-old chicks by feather as well as colour, dealing with thousands of chicks each week, leads me conclusively to the opinion that these principles are to all intents and purposes 100% correct in practice.

Colour patterns

Colour patterns can be classified into the following five groups in order of dominance:

1. Self or spread pattern
2. **T** pattern or **T** Chequer (tail bar)
3. Ordinary Chequer
4. Barred
5. Barless

A pair of birds of the same pattern cannot produce the pattern above them in the table, but they can produce the pattern below; e.g. a pair of Blue Bars cannot produce a Chequer, but a pair of Chequers can produce a Bar.

The **T** pattern or **T** Chequer has a tail bar and is the equivalent of the Velvet of the Racing Homer, although in the

48

West with its white tail this factor cannot be used to identify the pattern, but many of the broken or off-colours (barless Strawberries, Mealies or Lavenders) would come into this group.

The Barless pattern has no bar on the tail and, in my opinion, is rare in Wests. The only way to identify patterns correctly is to mate a pair of birds together and compare the resulting progeny.

Dominant and Recessive Colours

There are two types of colour — intense and dilute — and the intense colour is always dominant to the recessive dilute colour. Intense colours are Red, Mealy, Black and Blue; and dilute colours are Yellow, Cream, Dun and Silver.

The order of dominance is:
1. **Red** and **Mealy** are dominant to all other colours.
2. **Black** and **Blue** are dominant to all colours except Red and Mealy.
3. **Cream** and **Yellow** are dominant to Dun and Silver.

Red or Ash Red is a dominant colour so a pure Red cock when mated to other colours will give all Red progeny, but if the cock is impure (i.e. carrying genetically a factor for a second colour) then both colours can be produced in the progeny of either sex.

Sex-linkage

The sex of a bird is determined by two special sex chromosomes out of its full chromosomal complement, which are called **X** and **Y** chromosomes. Cocks have two **X** chromosomes and hens have one **X** and one **Y** chromosome.

Every chromosome is composed of a number of genes strung together, each of which determines a factor in the bird's make-up. In Wests it is believed that the genes for colour are located on the **X** chromosomes, hence the term "sex-linked"

49

related to colour.

In the breeding process each parent transmits one sex chromosome to each offspring. So if a dominant colour is carried by the hen on her one **X** chromosome this will be linked with an **X** chromosome from the cock (he has only **X** chromosomes so there is no choice) so that the resulting dominant coloured bird must be a cock. If the cock is pure for his colour, the hens produced by this mating will be of his colour, or if he is impure, they may be the colour which he carries genetically as a recessive factor.

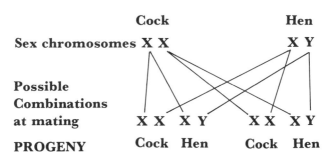

PARENTS

PROGENY

A Red (or Barred Ash Red or Mealy) hen mated to a Yellow cock will always produce Red (or Mealy) cocks and Yellow hens, and likewise Black or Blue hens mated to their dilute Dun or Silver cocks. It also applies when colours other than the related intense and dilute forms are mated together, so that, for example, a Red hen will produce Red cocks when mated with Black, Blue, Dun, Silver or Cream cocks.

It is probable that Silver is recessive to all other colours; it is particularly difficult to get a Silver cock — in one well-known breed I believe that there has been only one bred in the last decade. Here again, if a Barred cock, e.g. Cream, is mated to a Silver hen and all the progeny are Cream, then the cock is pure for Cream, but if any Silver hens are bred then the cock is impure and carries the Silver factor, and could therefore be used to try to produce a Silver cock.

Some people say that they have bred colours or patterns which cast doubts on these principles, but my firm belief is that this does not occur in single pen matings, but in the average loft where more than one pair are mated such unexpected results could be put down to cross-mating. There is also the fact that a bird may not be genetically just the colour which is visible to the eye. Inbreeding Red Prints can, in a few years, produce a White Self, but these birds are still genetically dominant Ash Red, pure in the case of a hen, but pure or impure in the case of a cock.

Because a hen has only one **X** chromosome she can only carry her own colour but she can also carry the factor for Bars; an impure cock, with two **X** chromosomes, can also carry a recessive colour plus the dilutes plus the Bar factor. For example, if an impure Red cock carrying the factor for Black is mated to a Red hen the progeny could be Black, Blue (if the Bar factor is also carried), Mealy, and Cream (dilute of Mealy), Silver (dilute of Blue) and Dun (dilute of Black). The Reds and Mealies could be cocks or hens, but all other colours must be hens, since only the **Y** chromosome which does not carry the dominant Red has been transmitted to them by the parent hen.

As well as the dominant Ash Red of the West and most other flying breeds, there is a recessive Red in breeds like the Long-faced Tumbler, but this is not found in the West. In flying breeds such as Racing Homers and Cumulets, White is very often a dominant colour — usually a faded Red — hence the red hackle

Figure 3.2 **Cream Bald cock. Bred and exhibited by the author; now the property of Mr. G. Richer, Colchester. 1st and Clayton Trophy, Best Young Bird: West of England Flying Tumbler Society CH Show, Bideford; 1st and N.P.A. Certificate, Best West: Burry Port CH Show.**

often found in young Cumulets.

Lavender is not sex-linked in some fancy breeds. So-called Lavenders in Wests are usually faded Strawberries and so genetically they are Ash Red dominants.

A Table of Sex-linked Colour Matings			
Parents		Progeny	
Cock	Hen	Cocks	Hens
Yellow	Red/Mealy	Red/Mealy	Yellow
Cream	Red/Mealy	Red/Mealy	Cream
Black	Red/Mealy	Red/Mealy	Black
Blue	Red/Mealy	Red/Mealy	Blue
Dun	Red/Mealy	Red/Mealy	Dun
Silver	Red/Mealy	Red/Mealy	Silver
Dun	Black	Black	Dun
Silver	Black	Black	Silver
Yellow	Black	Black	Yellow
Cream	Black	Black	Cream
Dun	Blue	Blue	Dun
Silver	Blue	Blue	Silver
Yellow	Blue	Blue	Yellow
Cream	Blue	Blue	Cream
Silver	Cream	Cream	Silver
Dun	Yellow	Yellow	Dun

As the Bar factor is not sex-linked, Mealy instead of Red cocks and Blue instead of Black cocks may be produced if the Red and Black hens are carrying the Bar factor and if the cock is Barred or is carrying the factor for Bar.

If the cocks in the above table are not pure, say a Cream bred from a Cream/Silver mating so that the cock is a Cream carrying Silver as a recessive factor, then the hens may be of the recessive colour that the cock is carrying, in this example, Silver.

Mutations

Some fanciers, who are sceptical about the validity of breeding principles, may ask the $64,000 question. They will say that as Darwin said that all pigeons evolved from the Blue Barred Rock Dove, how is it that a pair of Bars (say Blues) cannot produce a Chequer or Self colour?

Well, Darwin himself, who used pigeons extensively in his research, was subjected to a great deal of scepticism about his theories, and much abuse was heaped on him when his great work *On the Origin of Species* was first published — even George Bernard Shaw referred to him sarcastically as "just an enthusiastic pigeon fancier".

The basic truth is that in evolution we are considering change which has taken place over millions of years, and even in the case of the domesticated pigeon the changes, both natural and man-assisted, have taken thousands of years.

Out of all those matings, one in a thousand or even a million has resulted in what geneticists call a **mutation**, which means that the offspring produced do not conform in every respect to the expected pattern. Many mutations result in undesirable characteristics, such as deformities of body or feather, or may even be lethal, but some mutations will arise giving good and desirable characteristics and it is by breeding from these birds, whether in the wild or in man-controlled situations, that new strains or varieties have arisen. It must be stressed, however, that these are genetic "accidents", whether fortunate or unfortunate, and do not invalidate the breeding principles outlined earlier.

BREEDING METHODS

The three methods of breeding used are **Outcrossing**, **Line breeding** and **Inbreeding**. Outcrossing and Inbreeding are self-explanatory terms, and some breeders use both methods: even very close inbreeding, such as brother/sister mating, and outcrossing by purchasing a bird from a totally unrelated blood line.

Although many breeders are unwilling to practise close inbreeding and habitually use the outcross method, I would say that their fears are largely unfounded, for there are many studs with a closed flock or closed stud system using inbreeding or line breeding to a greater or lesser extent. Two successful breeders who have died in the last few years, one a breeder of English rabbits and the other of Black Rosecomb bantams, are said to have used no outside blood for over forty years. Both these studs were world famous and of only average size.

Line Breeding

I feel that an explanation of the line breeding system would be useful here. To take an example from poultry: we had a closed flock of pedigree Rhode Island Reds and Light Sussex for about twenty-three years with no outside blood whatever, and the system used was the "Bossert System".

Bossert was a little-known White Leghorn breeder from Cambridge who did sterling work for his breed during the difficult time of the late 1920s and the '30s when fowl paralysis and a high mortality rate were commonplace. His work was acknowledged by contemporary scientists and the Bossert method was included in the text books of the time.

The essential requirement is a minimum of three pens per breed; six pens will give greater scope but less inbreeding. The pens are labelled Pen A, Pen B and Pen C. Females always remain in the pen in which they were born. The best cock in Pen A is bred to Pen B; the best cock in Pen B is bred to Pen C; and the best cock in Pen C is bred to Pen A.

If six pens are used they are labelled **A1, A2, B1,** and so on, and the flocks are then bred by the best cock of A1 being mated to B1, and the best cock of A2 being mated to B2, and so on. After a few years you have inbred closed flocks; when you mate the two flocks together you will produce hybrids (the equivalent of the plant breeder's F1 hybrid). In poultry, white egg hybrids are generally the result of crossing two strains of White Leghorn. Most, but not all, brown egg hybrids are the result of crossing two breeds.

Chapter 4

HOUSING, MANAGEMENT AND FEEDING

HOUSING

In general terms, the simpler the loft the more efficient it will be, for both flying and exhibition birds. Two compartments are absolutely essential as a minimum. For most of the year one will be used for cocks and one for hens, but during the breeding season one will be for the adult pairs and the other for the young birds. I find that ten to twelve Wests in one loft is an ideal number to fly and exhibit, as birds keep in better condition than if they are housed in greater numbers.

The minimum size for a loft is 6 x 8 feet divided into two 6 x 4 feet compartments, but much better results will be obtained if the compartment size is about 7 x 5 feet.

My loft has two 8 x 4 feet indoor non-flying compartments for older birds or for bought-in birds which have not settled. The two outside flying lofts measure 8 x 6 feet, with a third one, which is 12 x 6 feet divided into two compartments each being 6 feet square. During the breeding season I provide nest boxes about 2 feet square made from tea chests, although they could, of course, be purpose built.

The ideal is probably a loft about 18 x 8 feet divided into three

6 x 8 feet compartments, with an entrance door in the rear of the middle compartment. This compartment may be used either as a food store or be subdivided into two further 6 x 4 feet compartments, so that if a few pairs of markings other than Balds are kept they could be housed there. This partition can be of laths or dowels fitted vertically so that the birds do not cling to them and so damage their flights or tails. For a temporary partition during the breeding season a piece of Netlon garden netting could be used. If costs have to be kept down, this compartment could be reduced in size to a width of 3-4 feet.

This type of loft is suitable for both fanciers who fly their stock and for those who don't. The latter can at times have problems with birds which try to escape, but this sort of arrangement can help to prevent this because the door into the centre compartment can be closed before the partition doors are opened.

Materials

The loft may be constructed of horizontal weatherboards, shiplap or even external quality plywood at least $\frac{1}{2}$ inch thick and fixed to vertical studs. Any of these materials are better than the commonly-used tongued and grooved boards on horizontal framework because that type of construction provides ledges for the birds to cling to. If you find that your loft has such ledges, it is advisable to fix strips of plywood or something similar at an angle of 45-60° to keep the birds off. Even cardboard strips could be used as a temporary measure or where costs have to be kept right down. The partition walls of the two end compartments should be solid so that the cocks cannot see the hens when they have been separated.

No window frames are necessary if the top 1 foot at the front is left open and protected by laths or dowels and shielded from the weather by the roof overhang. In winter the space can be filled

Figure 4.1 **An ideal loft with staggered peg perches.**
A: **Plan of Loft**
B: **Cross-section through loft with penthouse roof, showing position of peg perches.**
C: **Cross-section through loft with span-roof showing position of peg-perches.**

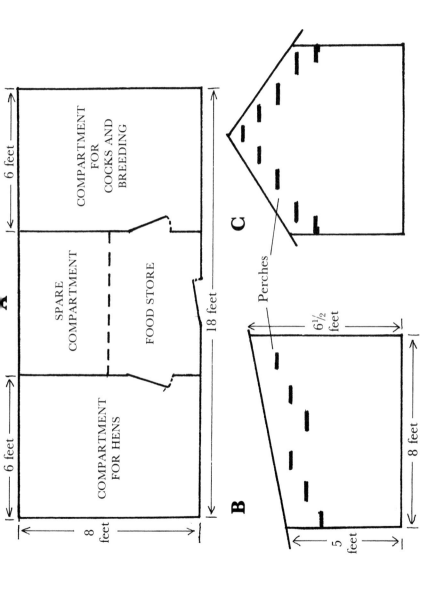

A

COMPARTMENT FOR COCKS AND BREEDING

SPARE COMPARTMENT

FOOD STORE

COMPARTMENT FOR HENS

6 feet

6 feet

8 feet

18 feet

B

Perches

6½ feet

8 feet

5 feet

C

61

in by frames covered with thick polythene or some other glass substitute leaving a ½ inch space at the top for ventilation. A fancier who flies his stock would fit shutters (see Chapter 5: Flying).

During the breeding season temporary nest boxes may be fitted in one of the end compartments. These can be constructed against the back wall by supporting shelves, 2 feet wide, on screws fixed in the partition and the outside wall. These shelves are then divided into suitable size nest boxes using partitions which will just slide into position. A size of 3 x 2 feet is required if the birds are to be confined until they have laid, but if they are only confined until they have settled down together, a box 2 feet square is sufficient. The front of the nest boxes may be fitted with laths or dowels.

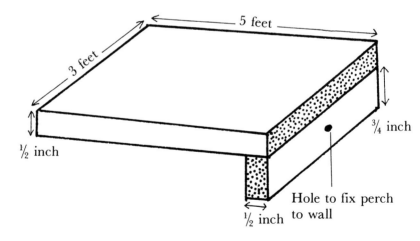

Figure 4.2 **Peg perch.**

Ventilation

Ventilation is extremely important for the wellbeing of the stock, and the best way to achieve it is to have an air gap of $\frac{1}{2}$ inch between the walls and the roof, and a sliding window covered with $\frac{1}{2}$ inch mesh wire netting which can be opened during really warm weather. Open fronted lofts with no other means of ventilation are not satisfactory: they are not ventilated unless the wind blows directly into the front, and they are very damp in winter unless well shielded.

Equipment

I find ordinary peg perches* the most satisfactory. They are constructed by nailing one piece of timber 5 x 3 inches to a second piece of timber 1 x 1 x 3 inches and then screwed to the walls of the loft. They should be spaced at least 12 inches apart or at 15-inch centres, and be placed at least 9 inches away from the adjacent wall so that the flight and tail feathers do not get damaged. It is also helpful to stagger the height of the perches. This not only allows droppings to fall clear of birds on lower perches but also acts as a guide to the fitness of the stock as the birds which are in better condition for the show pen will usually occupy the higher perches, although cocks tend to adopt a favourite perch. The number of birds which can be accommodated in a given area is less with peg perches than with box or saddle perches placed vertically above each other, but top honours have been won at championship shows all over the country by birds using this type; they may be taken straight from perch to basket with no pre-show preparation at all.

Box perches are favoured by probably the majority of pigeon fanciers. The usual size of each compartment is about 12 x 12 inches. The stack may be constructed of timber 4-6 inches wide and at least $\frac{1}{2}$ inch thick. If the 4-inch width is used, there will be

* **Also known by other names, including bracket perch**

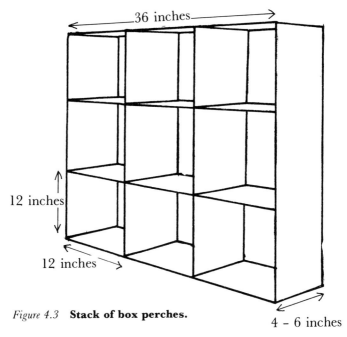

36 inches

12 inches

12 inches

4 – 6 inches

Figure 4.3 **Stack of box perches.**

less fouling to deal with, but there is obviously more danger of the birds on lower perches becoming fouled. The stack is fixed to the wall of the loft; it is advisable to leave a gap of at least $\frac{1}{4}$ inch between the wall and the perches so that wing or tail feathers cannot get caught in the joint. I find box perches unsatisfactory because they collect droppings and so need frequent scraping — I do not possess a scraper!

Saddle perches may be used either singly like peg perches or in a vertical stack as in Figure 4.5. If they are to be used singly they may be constructed from timber 4-6 x 5 inches and $\frac{1}{2}$ inch thick. If they are to be used in a stack it is preferable to use timber 7-8 inches wide in order to prevent the lower birds becoming fouled. It is advisable either to round the pointed ridge with a rasp or to fit a rounded ridge piece.

64

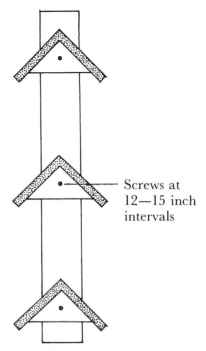

Screws at
12—15 inch
intervals

Figure 4.4 **Stack of saddle perches.**

Floor covering

Sand or, during the winter, a mixture of sand and sawdust are ideal for floor coverings.

Baths

One of the most important items of equipment is the bath. I find the most useful type is an ordinary galvanised bath about 2 x 1.5 feet and 9-12 inches deep. Give the bath once a week.

MANAGEMENT

The West is a very healthy breed and no trouble should be experienced as long as the management is sound. Various firms, such as **Harkers**, Lamberhurst, Kent, specialise in medicines and diagnostic services for the pigeon fancy, but fortunately I have never needed them as I have never known any illness or disease among the Wests in my loft, and such has been the experience of the majority of West fanciers.

Tonics and Conditioners

The older fanciers nearly always used Parrish's Chemical Food as an iron tonic, but this has gone out of favour because it has become too expensive. Those who would nevertheless still like to use it may like to consider the commercial form which is sold as ferrous phosphate.

A cheaper tonic may be made by making a solution of 1-2oz ammoniated citrate of iron in 1 pint of water. Use just enough of this solution to colour the drinking water lightly — the stronger the solution the less you need to use.

I make a ferrous sulphate solution in the same way, again using just enough daily to barely colour the water. Some fanciers' use about 1 teaspoon to 1 pint of water daily and others

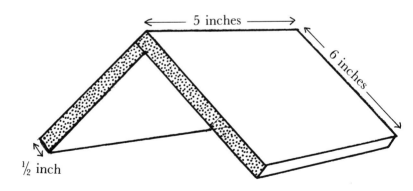

Figure 4.5 **Saddle perch.**

1 tablespoon to 1 pint two or three times a week.

A number of fanciers, particularly the younger ones, think that the older and consistently successful fanciers use secret tonics and seeds and will not divulge the information to others, but I don't think this is so; I find that most fanciers will talk quite freely about their methods.

One very successful fancier uses cider vinegar which can also be bought with added glucose. I have used 1 pint of this vinegar and 1oz ferrous sulphate to 1 pint of water in the same way as the iron tonic mentioned previously.

Today soluble vitamins are available in 50g bottles and are ideal for adding to tonics. If they are used during the breeding and exhibition seasons the birds are sure to be at peak fitness. A useful mixture consists of 1 pint of cider vinegar, 3oz ferrous sulphate and 50g multivitamins to 2 pints of water, given in the same manner as other tonics.

Cod-liver oil is valuable used in small quantities during the breeding and moulting seasons. Add no more than 1 teaspoon to 7lb of grain.

Parasites

It is essential that flying pigeons are kept free of all lice. Nearly all judges will disqualify a bird with pinholes caused by the large body louse which occur in the main flight and tail feathers. The long ticks which lie along the flights do not appear to cause any damage, but exhibiting birds with any "passengers" at all is a waste of time, money and effort. Moths are also said to damage feathers by nibbling them.

It is, then, absolutely essential to eradicate all forms of insect life in the loft, and to remember that re-infestation can occur at shows. Many people treat their birds before a show, but in my opinion this is a waste of time: they should instead receive attention on their return.

One method is to use *Duramitex* or Boots Poultry Mite Killer. This is applied as a coarse spray two or three times a year and is particularly effective against red mite. The birds are also dusted with a good insect powder or aerosol spray on their return from shows or at monthly intervals during the summer months.

Despite these precautions some fanciers claim that they still get lice infestation and are using Vapona fly strips after shows in addition to the other methods. One leading exhibitor claims that since adopting this approach he has had no problems at all with lice. He cuts a strip into three pieces and hangs one piece at each of his three compartments. Even though his lofts have a partly open front, this seems to do the trick. These strips have a life of three to four months and so they must be renewed promptly during the summer. It is certainly a lot easier than constant spraying. Fanciers who have tried ordinary fly sprays have found that they do not control lice; the active chemical in Vapona is the only substance which appears to work, so other brands of fly strip not containing this ingredient may not be as successful.

The Moult

A breeding pair should be separated by the end of May so that they can start on an early moult. The longer they are mated, the later the moult will commence; but if they start to drop their flights in May or June they should then have completed the moult in time for the classic shows which are held between October and December. Birds separated at the middle or end of May will probably have finished by the beginning or middle of October. Some birds, however, never seem to finish moulting until December no matter when they are separated, but this is usually an hereditary factor which runs in some families.

The birds drop their first (inside) flight to start with. When about half the flights have gone, the secondaries will start to moult. Later still, the tail feathers will be cast two at a time and the body moult will start.

After the bird has dropped its ninth flight it is wiser not to handle it and certainly wiser not to exhibit it. The last flight is very vulnerable to damage, whether still in the sheath or actually growing, because it is on the outside of the wing. Once this flight is three-quarters grown the bird can be handled again and exhibited, although it is really better to wait until the moult is completed since, at the classic shows in particular, there will always be one or two Wests which have completed their moult and so will take the top awards, even though they are equal in quality with your birds.

It can take one or two weeks after the last flight is finished for the bird to feel good in the hand. I have often felt when judging in October that a bird was not quite ready, and upon opening the wing found, sure enough, that the last flight had $\frac{1}{2}$-1 inch to go and that the bird had been exhibited two or three weeks before it was ready.

During the moult it is essential to avoid additional stress such as excessive flying or exhibiting and to make sure that the birds receive a full and balanced diet. Vitamins should be added to the water (see Tonics and Conditioners, above) and linseed and a few drops of cod-liver oil added to the feed. Any faults or checks will show themselves in poor quality flights or in frets in the feathers, although the latter can be another inherited fault.

FEEDING

This is probably the most important factor in maintaining birds in the right condition for either breeding, flying or exhibiting. Food should always be given in proper feed pots and grain kept safe from vermin in proper metal bins.

Grains

Barley has the lowest number of calories or energy and is therefore the least fattening, so it is surprising that it was used before the war to fatten poultry. The competition Flying Tippler fanciers were certainly aware of this fact at the beginning of the century; they knew that giving their birds a full feed would give them enough to fly on but not enough to put on any unwanted fat. Normally the youngsters were weaned on a wheat and barley mixture, then they progressed to barley on its own. I have heard fanciers say that if a Tippler could not fly for eight to ten hours on barley alone, then it was no good. The extra time which they can fly now is due to other foods, such as peas, maize and wheat, and various seeds being added to the diet in accordance with a strict training and feeding programme. Pigeons do not find barley particularly attractive, but it has its place, particularly in the flying loft.

Oats are of only limited value; the grains seem to be too long for the birds to enjoy even when they have been dipped.

Wheat is higher in energy but lower in protein than barley.

Dari and **Milo** are two introductions which may be used instead of wheat but not many pigeon fanciers use them.

Maize is higher in energy and lower in protein than all the other grains. Small grained or kibbled maize should be used. Some fanciers say that cut, split or kibbled maize causes canker, but although I have been using it all my life, I have never found this to be so.

Pulses

Maple peas and **beans** are very high in protein and seem to be the best food of all for maintaining body condition for the show pen. Racing Homer fanciers sometimes use them for as much as 75-80% of their feeds, especially before long-distance races. Although most fanciers use a mixture of peas and beans, some use only peas or only beans. One well known specialist, one of the very few with his own English named strain, once said that he doubted if he had used even 1 cwt of beans in the whole of his long career. Of the two I prefer maple peas and in particular Tasmanian maples. If Tic beans are fed, they should be as small as possible — the size known in the trade as **Minors**.

Tares may be fed instead of peas. They are high in protein and much smaller than peas, but are normally used only for very small pigeons or for the short-faced breeds which cannot manage peas or beans.

Feed mixtures

For flying, breeding and rearing youngsters:

   1 part maple peas
   1 part Tic beans
   1 part wheat
   1 part small or kibbled maize

Once the youngsters are weaned and also when adult hens are not feeding young, the maple peas can be replaced by Tic beans but more youngsters seem to be bred and reared when at least some of the beans are replaced by peas.

For summer shows:

   3 parts Tic Beans
   1 part wheat
   1 part maize

On this mixture the birds can be flown and will also do well in the show pen.

For winter classic shows:

   7 parts Tic beans
   2 parts maize
   1 part wheat

A good tip is to dry the corn in a moderate oven for at least an hour, using shallow dishes or trays and stirring the grains after half an hour. The older Game fanciers always fed split peas with a touch of wheat (again dried in the oven) to get their Old English Game and bantams really fit and hard for the classic shows of North Lancashire and Cumberland in the old days.

Seeds

Most fanciers use seeds of some sort as a tonic or pick-me-up. It may be plain **canary seed** given two or three times a week, and perhaps for a day or two before a show, or an equal mixture of canary seed and **linseed** given during the moult. You can buy both moult and show pen seed mixtures from most of the larger suppliers.

A mixture containing **hemp seed** is quite useful when hens are slow to lay in the cold weather early in the breeding season. A useful mixture for the moulting and breeding seasons contains:

> **2 parts mixed canary seed**
> **1 part hemp seed**

This mixture is added to the evening feed, one handful being sufficient for eight to ten birds.

Grits

In the old days it was common practice to give pigeons a box containing mortar rubble, but today most fanciers use a proprietary brand of pigeon grit. There are two kinds available. The first is insoluble and will not dissolve in water or body fluids, so it remains in the gizzard to help in crushing the grain. Usually these grits are of flint or granite; the latter is preferable as there are no sharp edges to harm the bird. The second type is soluble and is composed mainly of calcium which can be absorbed into the blood stream and thence into the organs and bones. Oyster shell and limestone grits are examples of this type.

Sometimes during hot weather birds are unable to absorb calcium as easily as they can in cold weather and consequently the hens lay eggs with thin shells or they may go off their legs temporarily after laying. The latter condition can also be due to extra pressure on a nerve during the egg forming and laying periods. The hen usually recovers quite rapidly, but if the cock-bird is over-active it may be necessary to fasten the hen in a nest box for a day or so.

In addition to the grits, some fanciers place in the loft a small quantity of garden soil in a box. The birds will peck at this, presumably picking up valuable trace elements. Some people hang up green food or chop up finely extra tit-bits like lettuce, cress or dandelion leaves.

Figure 4.6 **Drinker and Food Hopper.**
Left: **Pigeon Drinker** *Right:* **Food or Grit Hopper**

Water

It is essential that the birds should have access to a supply of clean water in non-foul drinkers.

Chapter 5

FLYING

One of the greatest pleasures in keeping a dual-purpose breed like the West lies in cultivating its high-flying ability. When weather conditions are right, any West worthy of the name should be able to fly so high that it looks like a butterfly, and after that soar to such great heights that it becomes a mere speck or even disappears from sight completely. The flying movement is known as a *butterfly action*: a slow, deliberate movement with the wings well spread and the tail slightly spread.

THE FLYING LOFT

The loft can be fitted with one of the many types of trap available, or with a simple alighting board, with either a small opening fitted with bob-wires or a larger shutter or window covering an opening at least 2 feet x 1 foot, 6 inches.

My own flying lofts have a shutter or window over an opening 3 feet x 2 feet with a hinged alighting board 3 feet square. The windows and shutters slide from side to side to allow plenty of room for the birds to leave and return to the loft with no risk of damage to their feathers.

Figure 5.1 **The author's flying lofts.**

Settling Young Birds

In my opinion it is not wise to try and break adults to a new loft. They should be used for breeding and their offspring flown from the time they are weaned.

There are three methods of settling young birds. The **first is to do nothing**. In time the birds will find their own way on to the loft roof and take to the air. The **second method** is to wean the youngsters at four to five weeks and then put them in the young bird loft. Leave them for a day to settle in, then on the second day place one or two on the alighting board. The rest will soon follow and in a couple more days will be flying in and out of the loft. The next step is to carry one or two birds a few yards from the loft and then allow them to fly back. Some fanciers use a platform a few yards from the loft and get the young birds to fly to and fro.

76

Once the birds are used to alighting on the board or loft roof they can be coaxed on to the wing, but it does not matter if only some of them take to the air. These training sessions should be carried out every day; it is a mistake to let them lapse at this stage so, unless the wind or weather are really terrible, try to let them out every evening. It is also advisable at this time to keep the birds slightly hungry and, if feeding *ad lib*, to remove the food after lunch.

With the **third method**, the birds are left alone, as in the first method, until you are sure they have all been in the air and are fairly well used to the loft. Then they can be coaxed or driven off, as in the second method.

The principal aim in flying youngsters is to get them really used to the loft; they need not necessarily be expected to fly really high for weeks or even months and, in the case of late hatched young, their true flying ability may not become apparent until after the breeding season of the following year.

Flying Older Birds

Old birds will not fly very high or for very long during the breeding season. Once this is over, when the sexes have been separated, then real high flying can begin.

One mixture for breeding, weaning youngsters and flying has already been given in the section on Feeding in the previous chapter. Another good mixture is:

3 parts peas
2 parts wheat
1 part maize

On this, Wests will fly high for up to three hours and they will keep in sufficiently good body condition to be exhibited at the summer shows.

During the winter it is advisable to increase the proportion of peas in the mixture and to increase the quantities given at each feed. This will have two results: the body condition of the birds will be improved still further for the classic shows, and the height and time flown will be restricted, thus safeguarding against the flyaways which can be brought about by the vagaries of the winter weather. In my locality, for instance, during the winter months the sea mist can come sweeping in without warning on the clearest and brightest of days.

What greater pleasure can there be than to see your kit of Wests flying really high on a summer's evening and to know that they are at the same time birds of a quality able to hold their own in the pen at the classic shows.

Chapter 6

JUDGING AND EXHIBITING THE WEST

QUALITIES OF JUDGES

As the West is a non-standard flying breed it is essential that at the top shows which have championship status, the judging should be undertaken by someone who is recognised as a good judge of a flying pigeon and can assess the West on a combination of type, handling, feather and condition, treating these factors as of the utmost importance and placing less emphasis on minor points such as colour, markings, or grouse-muffs.

A good judge will not disqualify for slight faults. Obviously, though, these minor points must be taken into account if there are two exhibits which cannot otherwise be separated, and of these the eye is probably the most important because historically Tumblers have always had pearl or white eyes.

Some judges adopt a system of fault judging, particularly in large classes, simply eliminating birds for particular faults, some of them of little significance. This is frowned on in most livestock judging circles, but unfortunately is accepted among pigeon fanciers. It is often responsible for mediocre birds being placed ahead of birds which are superior in the important aspects. Judges who use this method say that disgruntled exhibitors have almost forced it upon them, since the only way to silence some of them is to tell them that their bird has failed because of a fault in the eye, for example, or a fret in its feather, or a clipped flight.

It is absolutely essential when judging to put out of your mind all personal preferences for colour or marking, and to mark all the exhibits as though they were your own.

JUDGING POINTS

Shape   There is a variety of opinion on the ideal shape, as can be seen in the comments recorded at the end of Chapter 2. The type described in the *Fulton Book of Pigeons* must be understood to relate to all Flying Tumblers. The majority adopted *Standards* and from there developed into the Muffed and Clean-legged, Long-faced Tumblers of today.

The term "apple-bodied" is widely used, but I feel that "pyramidal", "pear-shaped" or "egg-shaped", which are used by some English and many continental fanciers, are much more descriptive of the shape when the bird is held in the hand.

Legs   Tipplers are required to be low on the leg: according to the older fanciers, there should be just enough leg to carry the leg ring. The West, however, should have a leg of medium length with the hock bent to give the upright, jaunty, "ready to fly" look which is typical.

Head   There are two slightly different types, but I would not differentiate between them when judging. The first type is the true flying pigeon head with a rather prominent forehead (the brainbox, according to some old fanciers!) with just enough curve over the eye to avoid a flat top to the head. Unfortunately, some of the younger and less experienced judges penalise them for being square or blocky.

The second type is a rather full oval, "pleasant-faced" or

dove-shaped head, rising gradually from the wattle, nicely curved over the top of the eye and blending well into the neck.

ACCEPTING THE JUDGES DECISION

Judging is a thankless task and, while there is nothing wrong in asking the judge why your exhibit has failed, every exhibitor must learn to accept defeat gracefully and must certainly never abuse the judge or question his awards. If you are a bad loser you may as well pack the game in straight away. In law there can be no objection to a decision based on the judge's assessment of merit. The only possible ground for an objection is if a bird has been wrongly classed.

ADOPTION OF STANDARDS

Some of the less experienced West fanciers feel that all breeds should have *Standards*. This ignores the historical fact that all Flying Tumbler breeds for which *Standards* have been adopted have changed into Muffed or Clean-legged, Long-faced Tumblers over a period of time, and if these West fanciers really want to have *Standards* they should turn to one of these.

The adoption of a *Standard* for Flying Cumulets, a beautiful high flier, has done nothing for the breed: it is now at a low ebb and appears to be heading for extinction. Three attempts between the 1890s and 1920s to produce a *Standard* for the Racing Homer have resulted in the Show, Exhibition and Genuine Homer respectively.

Figure 6.1 **The ideal bird.**
1. Grouse or Trumpet Muffs — these should be 1 - 1½ inches long.
2. Flights — ten in number.
3. Secondaries — ten in number.
4. Shoulders — these should be prominent, broad and strong.
5. Eye — these should have small, black pupils and broad white or clear pearl irises.
6. Eye Cere — this should be fine, silky and flesh coloured.
7. Wattle — this should be small, neat and also flesh coloured.
8. Beak — this should be long and flesh coloured.
9. Gullet — this should be free from any dewlap.
10. Chest — full and broad.

M E PRINGLE
1980

EXHIBITING

It cannot be said too often that, if it were not for the show pen, the West would not exist as a distinct breed of high-flying British pigeon; they would all be various strains of what is generally known as "Tumbler-type" competition Tipplers. I do not know of any strain of West able to trace its ancestry back to the old days that is flown and not exhibited. Its survival during the Depression of the 1930s and World War II was entirely due to a handful of dedicated fanciers who either exhibited only or exhibited *and* flew their Wests.

SHOWS

Summer agricultural shows, which normally schedule one or two classes for the breed, start off the show season. One or two shows, such as British Timken and Blackburn, schedule four classes and are commonly regarded as summer classics.

Classic shows are those regarded as leading shows for the breed and usually schedule eight classes: four classes for Red, Yellow, Strawberry, and Mealy, and four classes for any other colour. A list of shows is given in Chapter 7.

Ringing

Before being exhibited all birds must be rung with either a West of England Flying Tumbler Society or a National Pigeon Association ring. Full details may be found in *Pigeon and Pigeon World*.

Show Preparation

It is essential when you have what you consider to be good typical specimens, well feathered and strong flying types, that you pen them in as good condition and as clean as possible. It is

84

JUDGING AND EXHIBITING THE WEST

better to leave your choice of exhibits to the last minute, basing it on their condition on the day of the show.

If birds have been fed and managed as outlined in Chapter 4, then you will only need to increase the quantity of peas to at least $\frac{2}{3}$ of the ration, and to give a little seed, such as canary seed, and an iron tonic two or three times a week.

Give them the bath three or four days before the show, adding enough laundry blue to the water so that it is coloured such a deep colour that you cannot see the bottom of the bath. After the bath do not handle your birds until you make your choice before basketing.

No other preparation should be necessary. When you exhibit Wests you show what God or Nature has produced and take the bird straight from perch to basket.

Travel

If you are sending your birds by rail use a light basket to save costs. Wests should always travel in proper baskets with separate compartments. Put a couple handfuls of wood chips into each compartment.

Always handle your birds carefully, stroking the folded wings and tail before basketing and again when penning, whether you are dealing with your own or another fancier's birds.

Selecting Exhibits

I am not in favour of trying to exhibit birds which you think will appeal to a particular judge. In a different field, I well remember many years ago showing an Alsatian bitch under a famous breeder and championship show judge. In duplicate classes of over twenty championship-winning Alsatians I won 1st, 2nd and 3rd. A few weeks later the same judge was at a smaller show. My bitch was in better condition then ever so I entered her in what was a terrible entry of only four, five and six entries per class, and terrible specimens at that: long-haired, leggy, soft ears, the lot. I came last in every class. In pigeons the same thing happens and since condition varies from week to week the effect can be even more pronounced.

Always back your own judgement. Look for perfection along the lines described in Chapter 2, recognising that while it is a will-o'-the-wisp and unattainable, a really top winner should be as near perfect as possible on all points. It may be marred by minor blemishes, but that is as near perfection as we ever get.

Of the four attributes considered by good judges to be important (type, condition, handling and feather), condition comes top of the list. If a bird fails in this the judge will pop it back in its pen and it will have no chance of an award.

WAITING FOR MATURITY

Compared with breeds like Tipplers and Rollers, the West is a slow maturer. It is often difficult to assess even early hatched young birds until October or November. You will, of course, be able to eliminate as unsuitable a proportion of your young stock quite early in the season, but a bird which appears then to be only a good average may well emerge by the end of the year as a top-notcher.

Some cocks may not reach their best until they are three years old — some older fanciers would say five years. Hens mature earlier and may be at their best as yearlings. West fanciers certainly need the virtue of patience, but unfortunately many present-day fanciers seem always to be in a hurry, lacking the perseverance necessary to attain long-term objectives.

When I decided to produce my own strain of Red Spangle Wests I started with a Red Oddside. It took three years to produce a good Spangle hen which won her class at Harrogate. The next year this hen produced another good hen which won her class at Bideford, but I had not so far produced a Spangle cock. The next year I did produce a good one. Unfortunately, it was odd-eyed, but the following year I produced an excellent cock with good eyes. It had taken six years to produce two good pairs of Red Spangles.

Shows are places where fanciers can meet to discuss their hobby and this is one of the best facets of our wonderful hobby. May you have as much pleasure as I have in flying and exhibiting our wonderful dual-purpose West of England Flying Tumbler.

Chapter 7

ORGANISATION

The main bodies of the Pigeon Fancy affecting the West of England flying Tumbler are as follows:

National Pigeon Association Secretary: H. Wheeler, 66 Curzon Street, Reading, Berks.

This is the governing body of the pigeon fancy except racing pigeons. N.P.A. rings are issued each year from 18 January to 31 July to members only. The current annual subscription is £2. When birds change hands, the transfer must be registered; the fee for this is 15 pence.

Wests, Flying Tipplers and Birmingham Rollers may be rung with either an N.P.A. ring or a ring from any affiliated club or governing body catering for the three breeds of High Flyers, the collective name for our three native flying breeds.

The West of England Flying Tumbler Society is run in conjunction with the Bideford and South West Flying Tippler Society. President: T.J. Hetherington. Vice-Presidents: L. Rubery, J.E. Johnson and J. Oldham. Secretary: P. Holland, 2 Coxleigh Cottages, Shirwell, Barnstaple, Devon.

The current annual subscription is 50 pence and rings cost 50 pence for ten.

Bristol Tippler and Tumbler Show Society. President: J. Oldham. Vice-President: J.E. Johnson. Secretary: H. Heal, 7 Carisbrooke Road, Knowle, Bristol 4.

The current annual subscription is 50 pence.

Norwich Flying Tippler and Flying Tumbler Society President: J. Oldham. Vice-President: J.E. Mullan. Secretary: M.F. Hopes, 36 Irstead Road, Norwich, Norfolk.

The current annual subscription is £1.25. Rings cost 50 pence for ten.

SHOWS

All three societies hold championship shows during the winter classic show season when about 200 of the finest Wests in the country are penned. Average entries may be as high as twenty to thirty per class. First prizes at all of them are about £1 — Bideford pays £1.50 for first place and £1 for second prizes. In addition a host of trophies and other specials are offered.

The W.E.F.T.S. Midlands Branch holds a show in conjunction with the Three Counties Show at Malvern each June, and the Northern Branch holds one with the British Pigeon Show Society's championship show at Doncaster in November or December. Last year the Eastern Branch held a show with the Sufex Championship Show at Colchester towards the end of October.

Wests are included in all the N.P.A. Championship Shows. For the 1979-80 season these were reduced to twelve spaced out around the country: Barnstaple and Swansea in the West and Wales; Reading in the South; Sufex and Norwich in the East; Northampton and Cambridge in the Midlands; Lancashire and Doncaster in the North; and Airdrie and Newcastle for the

North-East and Scotland. These shows all had championship status and were held between October and January.

The only summer championship show will be British Timken in August which normally attracts about 3,000 entries from all over Britain. At all these shows N.P.A. Challenge Certificates will be offered, one for each breed or sub-division of a breed. In order to qualify for the title of champion a pigeon must win three Certificates under three different judges, winning at least one as an adult.